Harvest

Kelli Lynn

Copyright © 2018 Kelli Lynn

All rights reserved.

ISBN: 0692124497
ISBN-13: 978-0692124499 (BAMF Books)

My poetry is an informal practice through which I meet the parts of myself I most need to remember and release. Welcome to this compilation of missing pieces, my first harvest.

This collection is dedicated to you.

CONTENTS

1. For My Son (1)
2. And For My Daughter (2)
3. Elegy to My Twenties (3)
4. Salt (4)
5. Seasons of Psychosis (5)
6. Last January in Washington (9)
7. After the March (11)
8. My Revolution Begins at the Laundromat (12)
9. When Heather Died (14)
10. Evolution (15)
11. Aya (19)
12. Women's Lodge (21)
13. The Festival at Night (22)
14. Allies (24)

All children grow into adults who will question every aspect of their identity and reach multiple conclusions. As you continue to experience life, you will form a variety of relationships, each of which has its own value and ideally brings you closer to understanding and appreciating your own self-worth. Remember, the goal is not to live happily ever after with your one true love forever, but to share your life with people who help you feel authentic, empowered, and whole. -KL

"A New Humanist Take on the Emerging Vocabulary of Romance, Gender & Sexuality," *The Humanist*, Feb. 2016

For My Son

The keeper of all the secrets,
you wait in the silence of the night,
one tiny hand resting gently on your belly,
the other curled up but for two fingers,
stuck squarely in your mouth.

In four years, you say so little:

I love you. I see you.

Come on! Let's go!

There it is. It's mine.

Sorry, Sissy. Thank you, Mama.

Happy boy.

The doctors say
Autism Spectrum Disorder
with developmental delays.

You just take my head in your hands and smile.
You know it is more important
we run really fast and leap,
feeling our weight upon the wind.

And for My Daughter

I like the days when we are
Bodhisattvas drinking hot chocolate,
the moonlight a spotlight on you
singing your way
down city streets, up clock tower hill.

At 9 years old, you struggle to read,
but you know more than I did
back when I used to ride around alternating
my Precious Moments Bible with Stephen King
while my mother scouted suburbia for new homes.

You know exactly how to tell the evil clown,
Pennywise, to shove it,
while also stating clear and clean that life is
too big, beautiful and mysterious
to be the creation of one vengefully loving God.

You question. You feel. You know.

Visionary. Artistic. Insightful. Bold.

We both love the story about how,
when you were two,
clad in pink striped stockings,
and a black polka dot dress,
you seemed to vanish.
I panicked,
as you watched me from the playground,
beaming love into my confusion,
wondering why I couldn't see
you had no need to be saved.

Elegy to My Twenties

After the fire came and leveled the shop,
mushroom clouds reaching up around the wreckage
of the first month of my marriage,
my apartment filled with smoke,
rubble of my past life smoldering with the skeletons
of future dreams, melted machines,
littering the yard . . .

I arrived here:

The house almost just across the street,
the city park in between,
rumored spot of an old train station haunted mostly
by our family—living ghosts,
crafting portals to hope and regret.

The couch where I sit this morning writing
is where I spent last winter,
huddled beside a space heater,
unexpected snow falling,
fever shaking me while I read the self-told story
of Susannah Cahalan and how her brain caught fire.

On the topic of survival, she says something like this:

I am back, but I am changed.
It's unclear, whether for the better or worse.
Somehow, I am both more and less of who I'd been.

That may as well be me.

Salt

Some say it helps to align one's intention
with some cycle of nature,
but I AM that cycle,
my body the keeper of the tides,
which pull intentions off our tongues
like crystals, cut sharp and smooth.

Seasons of Psychosis

Last night, your lover dreamed of toys
moving in strange patterns across the ground.
She thought of ink blots and oracles,
spirits bringing us a message.

I told her: *No. It's the wind.*

I think sometimes that truth is
the most beautiful mystery,
as I marvel about what it means
to share a life with you.

I know the cycles sink our people unless
a great love sets them free,
and my ego is just large enough
to think it can actually contain
the storms wrought after war,
which shaped both your childhood
and this wider world of battlefields,
now consumed by memory and dust.

Where does war come from?

Eve Ensler's *Insecure At Last* once gave me
some answers:

Men who never learn to cry.

Men who cannot process loss.

Women who watch the men and never speak.

I still cannot tell if staying
makes me the heroine or the victim.

So, I paint myself as a pioneer,
or maybe Jezebel at the jukebox,
slow dancing my way through
the seasons of psychosis,
making a home
along the borderlines
of our personalities.

There, madness makes
room for sadness,
carrying within it hope,
a tender seed.

Slavery within the United States hasn't ended. It has simply changed form. People of color are essentially harvested from their communities daily to fuel an industrial complex which relies on prison populations for cheap labor to sustain a capitalist economy run primarily by rich, white men—who themselves are dehumanized by the very system they lead. The system feeds principally on fear, and the counter to that it not bravery but love. Call it incredibly hokey. This doesn't change its truth. -KL

"A NORML Mom Takes Not One Step Back," *Bugs, Books & Beauty*, April 2017

Last January in Washington

We are women, but that isn't why we march.

Immigration.
Education.
Racial inequality.
Healthcare.
The War on Drugs.
The Freedom of Expression.

These are some reasons.

The right to have the first and most valued say
when it comes to how
we plan our parenthood,
reform our prisons,
medicate ourselves,
choose our partners,
open our minds,
and relieve our bladders.

These are some reasons too.

Our voices whisper only
when we are keeping up the long con,
and that broke around the time
we woke to the idea that maybe
we'd victimized ourselves,
believing we weren't human after all.

Now is the time to remember
what it means to be human,
to release our versions
of our neighbors' stories,
to accept there is always another truth,
always another way to heal.

Agreement,
solidarity,
and feminism
all fail
in the face of compassion,
the centerpiece of this movement
to hear each other.
Yet women can lead this march still.

In the battle of Us vs. Them,
we are historically Other—
the darkness cast from Eden,
driving change,
exacting pain,
and freeing love,
the partners and real life creators of men.

Divided together,
we claim space and time
hold more power than money and authority,
and we march
because we are the mystery,
the living history of ourselves,
unfolding at our feet.

After the March

A few days later,
my mother frames a picture
from the local paper.
It shows a sea of pink in black and white,
we women making history.

My father says she voted Trump
but stands proud of us for whom
speaking up means more than security.

Maybe because I've never felt a threat so great
as the one I pose to myself,
I have grown from my mother's love
without the seeds of her fears.

When you save yourself from yourself,
anything is possible.
All sins are on the table,
moral judgment replaced
by natural consequences and personal fidelity.

I can no longer choose death and call it life.
I can no longer seek a God outside my heart.
I can no longer walk the streets of Washington DC
and think my government has more power
than the strangers against whose bodies
I have stood in protest—
fear, sorrow, anger and strength mounting
as we looked at the mothers of people
shot mercilessly by trusted officials and
said aloud those children's names.
Again. And again.

My Revolution Begins at the Laundromat

The original version of this poem appears on One Billion Rising, onebillionrising.org.

My revolution begins at the laundromat,
where the man on the phone
casually reveals his history of drug abuse,
and the other guy breaks from his conversation
long enough to give a half-cocked cat call
as I sashay by, basket of cupcake covered
blankets in my arms.

This gives him pause.

My motherhood is now apparent–
pieces of my identity piled up dirty, raw and real,
a more authentic type of beauty.

There is so much beauty here.

Beauty in the children laughing,
Beauty in how the parents leave and then return,
calmed by cigarettes and starlight,
their old cars a refuge from the chaos within.

The too bright lights beat down on rows
of contained floods, and it strikes me:
Poverty paints on layers which can be stripped away,
given space to wait and come clean.

My revolution happens here,
where we strangers stand watch over the clothes
as they spin into a spiraling blur,
falling back flat into the pieces of soft armor
in which we will take cover from this world.

We share our humanity.

We share our filth.

We share our space.

The simple act of washing means
we plan to keep going,
meeting head on another day,
another opportunity for change,
and wonder,
and heartbreak,
and desire.

My revolution happens when I remember
there is always something to celebrate,
and always something to grieve.

When Heather Died

We came to march again after Charlottesville--
my daughter and son at my side, their father ahead.
I have never been to war,
but the drumming reminded me
of some old battle,
the drive to fight brought back to life
from an era at rest.

My peers confront their fears
by threatening the Nazis and defacing the statues.
Meanwhile, I am trying to exorcise something
from the ground,
to summon up the blood shed
along the old Atlanta highways,
to paint the town red with the memory that
no one is innocent.

I marched that day to affirm my own peace,
which comes when I expose injustice,
demand accountability,
and declare I'm not afraid.

I. Am. Not. Afraid.

Evolution

Last year's revolutionaries now fail us—
their quaint apologies, landing
like snowflakes in a volcano.

Yes, ladies. There are no perfect leaders.

But there is a beautiful way to fall—
open,
remorseful,
humble,
compassionate,
strong.

You may go where your people go,
but do not take your stand beside a man
who claims that *anyone* is more or less
than human.

Tameka Mallory.

Carmen Perez.

Linda Sarsour.

Bob Bland.

Last year, we needed you.

This year, we need ourselves.

#MeToo

#TimesUp

#NeverAgain

These words help seed a forest—
where trees of knowledge grow free,
bearing the fruit of movements so much greater
than their creators.

It's been some time now since I've had the desire for religion's stories, not because I feel failed by them or because I lack a sense of hope—as my childhood self naively believed of agnostics and atheists. Rather, I no longer want to place my faith in stories crafted by ancient men. It feels inauthentic to me. . . My faith is instead in the process—by which I mean nature and its cycles, containing all humanity, the Earth, the universe and all that exists undiscovered beyond that. I have faith that the process makes things all right in the end. That its purpose is to heal. And that people will never really understand how this works but shouldn't stop trying. Our quest to understand is a key element of the process itself. -KL

"She is Wild," *Bug, Books & Beauty*, November 2016

Aya

A life requires patience.
So does a journey.
You wait in silence
while a shaman shakes a baton,
beats a drum,
invites animal spirits to stay if they will
and go if they must.

You wait in the darkness, usually,
stark still, usually,
feeling nothing at all until suddenly
bodies disintegrate into pixels,
neon snakes swallow their tails,
the story of yourself dissolves into abstraction.

There's a circle of ancestral insects.
There's your birth and death.
A flock of hummingbird wings.
Or nothing.

Nightmares rage replete with daemonic kindness.
And aliens land at last,
the purveyors of techno-erotic revolution,
reflections of your subconscious mind.

In any case, prepare to weep.
Trees are no longer trees after Ayahuasca.

At the same time,
they are only trees,
changing instead with your perception
of the other things—
birds, fruit, air, breath, and wind—
beating against what feels like your cheek,
bare beneath the moon,
a mask on the face of quantum reality.

I marvel:

How vulnerable and strong it is, this waiting.

Women's Lodge

I held space outside the lodge almost 5 years,
with children at my feet,
before one November I came alone
and stepped inside the fire which did not burn me.

We call ourselves the Stone People there,
where we gather with the cycling moons
to honor the Earth and our stories,
carried in the tears we shed and songs we shout
in the hot dark of the sweat lodge.

I think it's beautiful the way the women lift
the hot stones with a pair of antlers,
placing them in the center of the lodge,
anointing them with oil,
sweet grass,
and words spoken in native tongues.

I've learned the words mean,
"Welcome grandfather."
So I take a little delight when
the stones break open,
as though we're splitting apart the patriarchy.

That aside, each round has its own purpose:

Awakening. Healing. Remembering. Becoming.

All in honor of the higher power
I know as my soul.

The Festival at Night

I'm sitting in a vagina-shaped chair, consuming and comforting my body with a firm grip and a softness, almost like the real thing. I could stay here hours, transfixed by the towering inflatables, bobbing in the wind a few yards away at the edge of the field and the forest. But my body needs motion.

I stand up, subconsciously wondering if how I feel now is what it was first like to be a woman—mesmerized, but not immobilized, by the myths designed to at once keep us from, and introduce us to, our authentic selves—embodied by Eve, Ishtar, Isis, Brigid and the Disney princesses too.

I walk into the woods, which are dark except for a wave of disorienting light, speckled across the leaves like fireflies masquerading as fairies along a path leading only deeper into itself, the Bardo of the mind. In the Bardo, loyalty leads to blindness if you let it, so I am loyal to nothing except agnostic wonder. With a flick of my thumb against the flashlight in my pocket, the magic in the trees is only shimmering LEDs again.

I can also see I'm standing at a crossroads—between the field, the hills, the lake and a fire, burning deeper in the woods, around which people are gathered drumming. Walking toward the lake, I think of Ophelia.

One time in college, my friend Rachel and I wrote a paper about the women of *Hamlet*. Our theory was they all died because they could not handle the weight of being wrong, the oppression of stigma.

To quote something else I once wrote: *Stigma is attached to anything which separates us from what our society considers to be ordinary regarding our appearance, spiritual beliefs, medical choices, diet, general health, parenting preferences, sexual preferences, relationship dynamics, gender identity, race, financial standing, politics, employment, entertainment, education, morality, living environment, birth plans and death arrangements—to be brief. If you are different, prepare to be judged. If you are human, prepare to be judged.**

While Ophelia condemned herself in a trial by water, witches burned in trials by fire, their real life blasphemy the sin of being powerful women. Swallowed by the forest now, the lake behind me, flames light up the faces of the festival witches—wild, shirtless women, one's head shaved bald, sweat pouring down. Somehow, their fierce, fluid dancing seems to pull the song from the drummers, as it also powers the fire itself, consuming a tower of wood, stacked high by men. The remains will lie upon the ash like oracle bones tomorrow, cold beneath the morning sun, a map to creating new stories.

"The Arrow on My Arm," *Bugs, Books & Beauty*, January 2017

Allies

The story goes, my great-great-grandmother Viola
took her name from the flowers.
They say she was an orphan, raised mostly wild
beside the old mills of Alabama and along
the Georgia rivers, where she danced for sailors
before meeting her husband, a Cherokee.

Viola made local history when she opened a nursery,
tending seedlings to full bloom and sale.
My mother, and grandmother, had Viola's knack
for helping lovely things to grow.

In thirty-five years, a garden remains
a mostly foreign land to me, but the plants speak,
revealing their deep medicine,
asking for my advocacy,
nourishing and nurturing me whole.

Our relationship blossoms after the harvest,
when I take the plants and use them
in teas, tinctures, salves, supplements and smoke.
Extracting their essence, setting them aflame,
or swallowing them whole,
I am a reaper, doubling as the keeper of their legacies.

For me, this balance is holy—
every breath, every swallow, a sacrament,
the connection between plants and people
ripe with potential for grace.

NOTES

Specific reference to literary works, public figures & social events named in *Harvest* are listed here:

IT by Stephen King, Scribner (re-issue) 2016.

Brain on Fire: My Month of Madness by Susannah Cahalan, Simon & Schuster 2013.

Insecure At Last: A Political Memoir by Eve Ensler, Villard 2007.

Hamlet by William Shakespeare, Folger Library Shakespeare Edition, Simon & Schuster 1992.

Women's March on Washington, January 21st 2017.

While the Women's March made history as a peaceful protest calling for inter-sectional human rights and condemning the Trump administration, its leaders Tameka Mallory, Carmen Perez, Linda Sarsour and Bob Bland came under fire in February 2018 for their connection to the infamously anti-Semitic Nation of Islam leader Louis Farrakhan.

Heather Heyer, a 32-year-old human rights activist, was killed on August 12, 2017 when a car driven by a white nationalist supporter crashed into a crowd of protesters at a rally in Charlottesville, Virginia, USA.

#MeToo & #TimesUp are movements addressing an end to sexual misconduct & exploitation. #NeverAgain is a movement for common sense gun control.

Quotations from Kelli Lynn's narrative writing are included in *Harvest* with citations following each quotation.

Kelli Lynn's work appears in a variety of publications, including her blog *Bugs, Books & Beauty*. A founding member of the steel percussion company TerraTonz LLC, Kelli is also an active supporter of the National Organization for the Reform of Marijuana Law (NORML); The International Center for Ethnobotanical Education, Research & Service (ICEERS); The American Civil Liberties Union (ACLU); Amnesty International; Trees, Water & People; Fractured Atlas, The Order of the Good Death and Bring Change to Mind. Previously a 7th grade teacher, she currently homeschools her two children. If you enjoy her work, please support Kelli via Patreon and purchase her creations on Etsy at BAMFBoutique. *Harvest* is her first chapbook.

www.bugsbooksbeauty.blogspot.com

www.patreon.com/kellilynn

www.etsy.com/shop/BAMFBoutique

www.ingramcontent.com/pod-product-compliance
Lightning Source LLC
Chambersburg PA
CBHW070049070426
42449CB00012BA/3200